Baby Beboo Bear

बेबी बेबू भालू

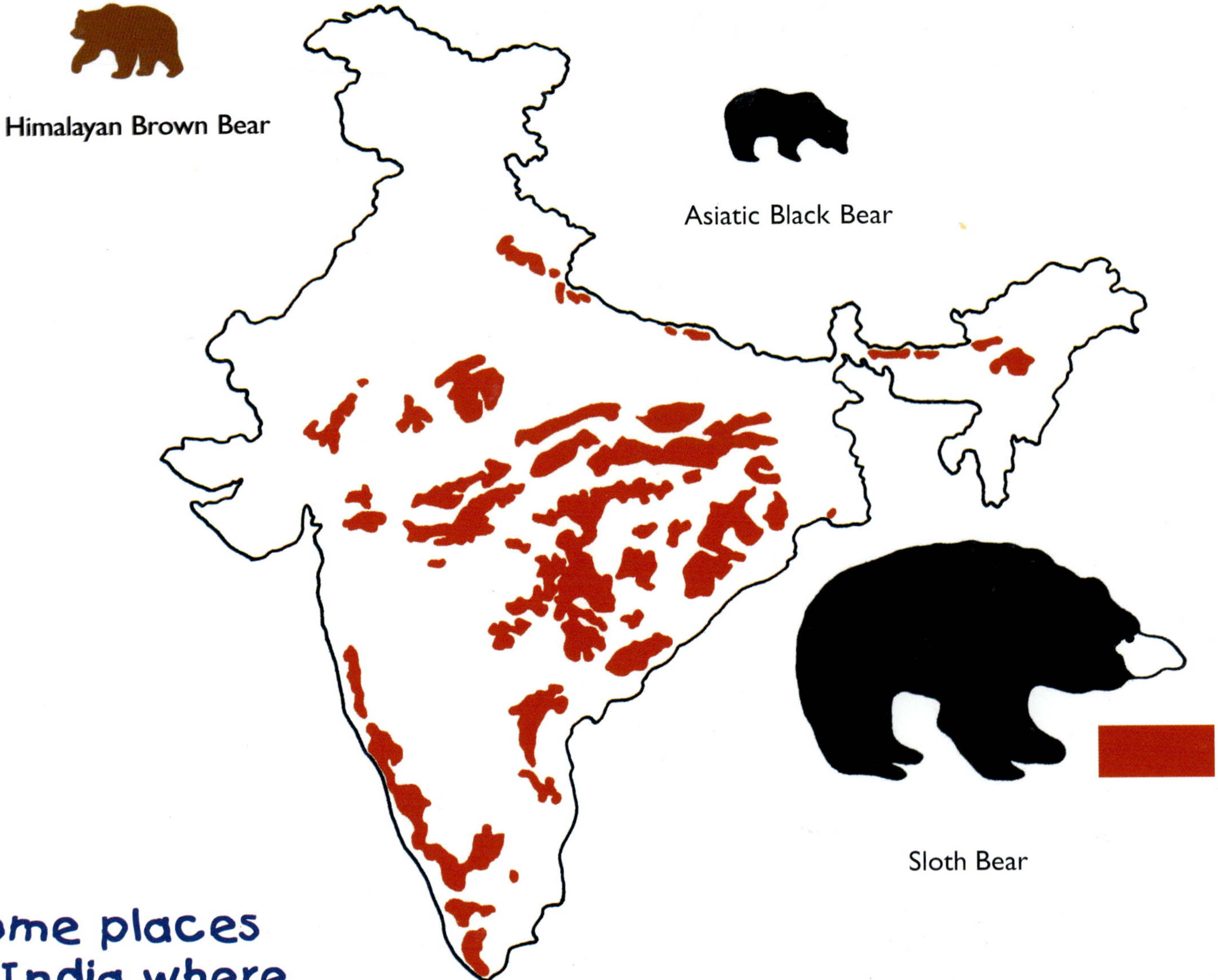

Some places
in India where
sloth bears are found

Tulika

Baby Beboo Bear

बेबी बेबू भालू

text and illustrations **Deepa Balsavar**
लेख व चित्र दीपा बलसावर

photographs **Wildlife S.O.S.** तस्वीरें वाइल्डलाइफ़ एस.ओ.एस.

translation **Sandhya Rao** अनुवाद संध्या राव

This book is dedicated to Bertie, Sneha, Kamala, Kartiyani, Giri, Suri, Keecha, Muskaan, Kitu, Dizi, Anandi and Pete... so that all the other bear cubs in the wild may have names given only by their mothers. — DB

Wildlife S.O.S. runs rescue centres at:

- Agra Bear Rescue Facility, Sur Sarovar Bird Sanctuary, Uttar Pradesh
- Van Vihar Bear Rescue Facility, Bhopal, Madhya Pradesh
- Bannerghatta Bear Rescue Centre, Bangalore, Karnataka
- Wildlife Rescue Centre, Vill Gopalpur, Gurgaon, Haryana
- Purulia, West Bengal

You can find out more about their activities at www.wildlifesos.org
Headquarters Wildlife SOS, D-210 Defence Colony, New Delhi, 110 024, India
Phone +91 11 46601096 / +91 9560011875
Email info@wildlifesos.org

Baby Beboo Bear / Baby Beboo Bhalu (English-Hindi)
ISBN 978-81-8146-480-4

First published in India, 2008
First reprint, 2023

Originally in English

Published by
Tulika Publishers, 305 Manickam Avenue, TTK Road, Alwarpet, Chennai 600 018, India
email reachus@tulikabooks.com *website* www.tulikabooks.com

Printed and bound at
SM Print, Chennai, India

Deep in the forest, little Beboo plays with her brother. Beboo is a sloth bear.

नन्ही बेबू अपने भाई के साथ घने जंगल में खेलती है। बेबू एक रीछ है।

They tumble and roll and wrestle with each other.

वे उठते-गिरते हैं और लुढकते हैं और एक दूसरे से कुश्ती करते हैं।

They romp about and climb and explore.

वे कूद-फाँदकर चढ़ते-उतरते हैं और छानबीन करते हैं।

Then, Mamma Bear says, "Come into the water, children. It's cool here!"

फिर मम्मा भालू कहती है, "पानी में आ जाओ बच्चो। यहाँ ठंड है !"

मुझे दीमक
बहुत पसंद हैं !

Mamma Bear shows her babies many things. She teaches them how to catch crunchy termites.

I love termites!

मम्मा भालू अपने बच्चों को खूब सारी चीज़ें दिखाती है।
वह उन्हें कुरकुरे दीमकों को पकड़ना सिखाती है।

She teaches them how to climb trees.

वह उन्हें पेड़ पर चढ़ना सिखाती है।

She teaches them where to find honeycombs and jungle bananas.

वह उन्हें शहद के छत्ते और जंगली केले ढूँढ़ निकालना सिखाती है।

Honey and bananas – my favourite foods!

Mamma bears are good teachers and cubs learn quickly.

मम्मा भालू अच्छी टीचर हैं और नन्हे भालू जल्दी ही सीख जाते हैं।

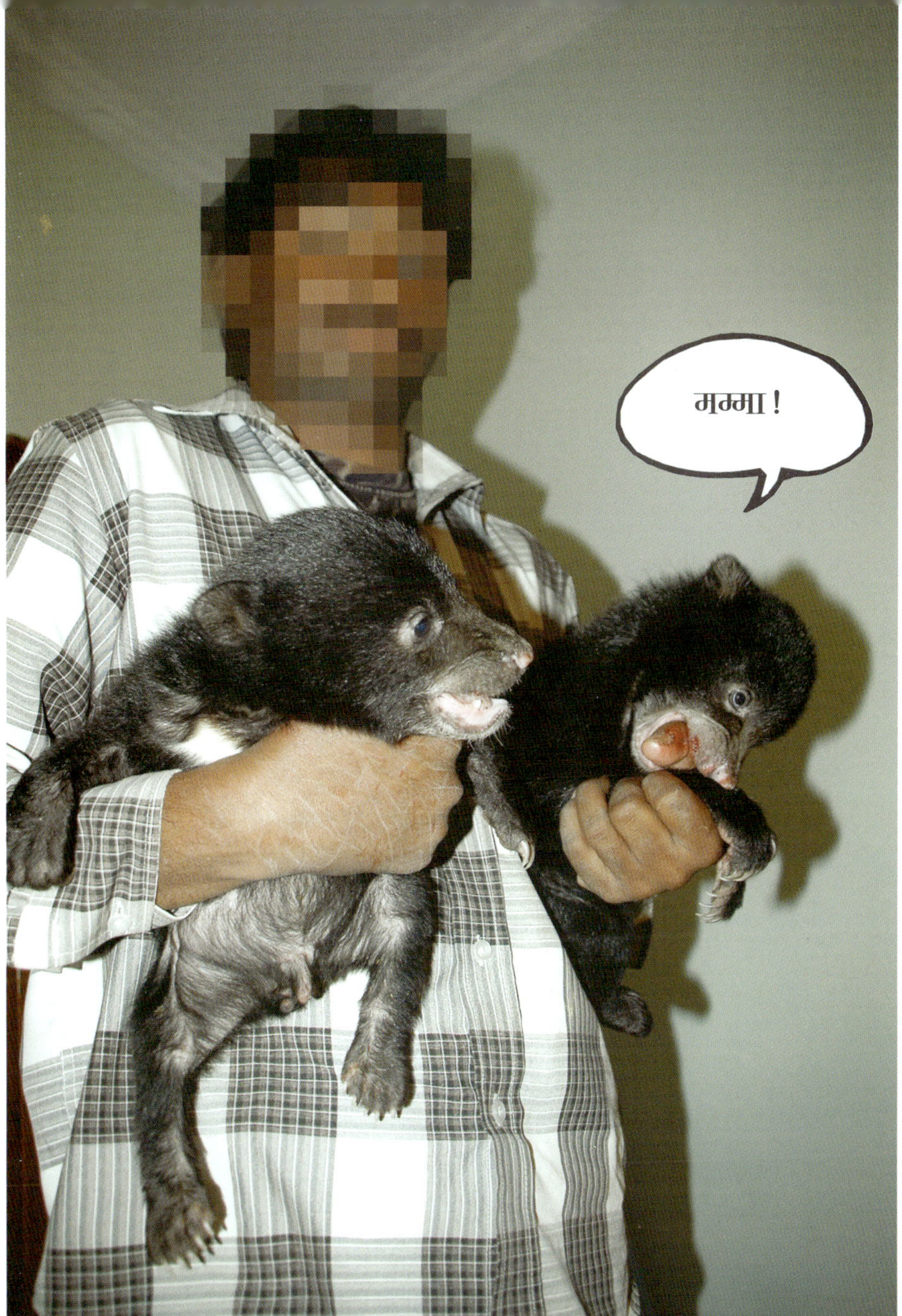

There is only one thing Mamma Bear is scared of. She is scared of men with sticks and nets who come at night to steal her babies.

मम्मा भालू बस एक चीज़ से डरती है। वह उन आदमियों से डरती है जो लाठी-जाल लिए उसके बच्चों को चुरा ले जाने रात को आते हैं।

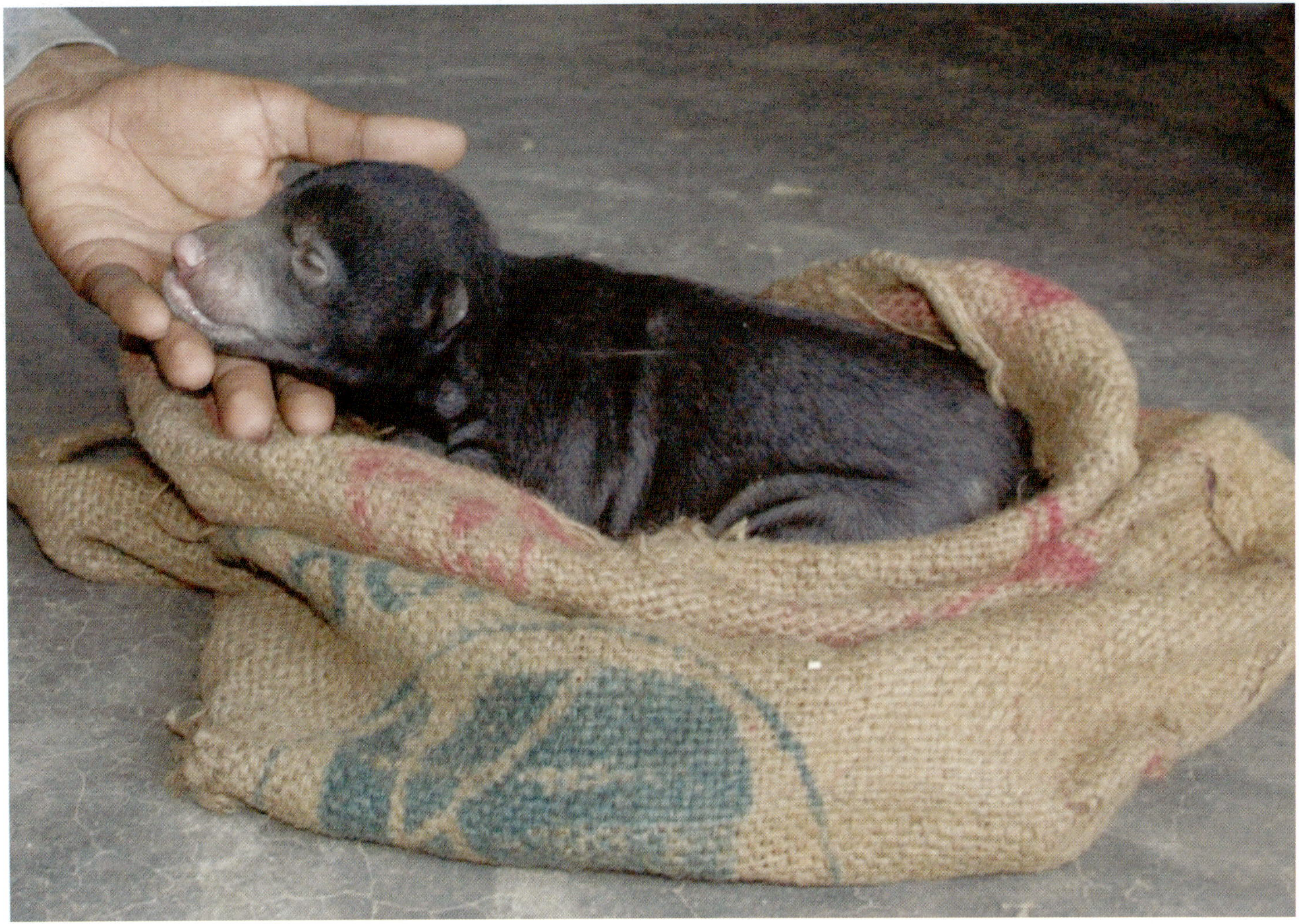

The babies are caught and put in sacks.

बच्चे पकड़े जाते हैं और बोरियों में डाले जाते हैं।

Then they are sold to the people who make them dance on the hot streets of towns and cities.

फिर वे उन लोगों को बेचे जाते हैं जो उन्हें नगरों और शहरों की तपती सड़कों पर नचाते हैं।

The bears that are caught look very sad.

पकड़े गए भालू बहुत दुखी नज़र आते हैं।

Holes are made in their noses and they are tied with rough ropes. This hurts the bears.

उनके नाक में छेद बनाए जाते हैं और उन्हें खुरखुरे रस्सों से बाँधा जाता है। इससे भालुओं को दर्द होता है।

Their teeth and claws are removed.
So they cannot eat properly or dig
for the termites they love so much.

उनके दाँत और पंजे निकाले जाते हैं।
इसलिए वे ठीक से खा नहीं पाते न ही
अपने पसंदीदा दीमक खोद पाते हैं।

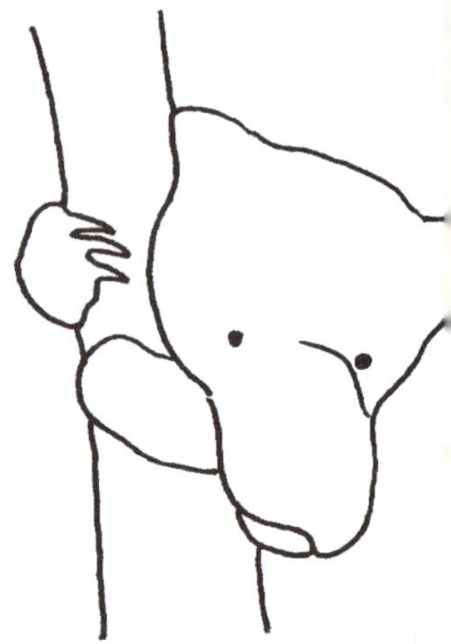

They are separated from their mothers and sisters and brothers.

वे अपनी माँ और बहनों और भाइयों से अलग किए जाते हैं।

Poor bears, thinks Beboo.
I will never let the men catch me!

बेचारे भालू, बेबू सोचती है।
मैं उन आदमियों की पकड़ में कभी
नहीं आऊँगी !

At the end of the day, Mamma Bear calls her babies into their little cave.

दिन ढलने के बाद, मम्मा भालू अपने बच्चों को अपनी छोटी-सी गुफ़ा में बुला लेती है।

It is time for bed. Good night, Beboo, good night little brother. Sleep well. You are safe now.

सोने का समय है। गुड नाइट बेबू, गुड नाइट छोटे भय्या। आराम से सोना। तुम अब सलामत हो।

Every year, over a hundred bear cubs are orphaned and poached after their mothers are killed, to be sold into the infamous bear dancing trade. Some cubs are barely six weeks old.

The baby bears are mutilated and beaten into submission. They spend their lives in pain and deprivation, made to perform for the entertainment of people.

Rescued bears are severely traumatised and disfigured and cannot be released back into the wild.

Wildlife S.O.S. is an organisation that helps rescue dancing bears and rehabilitate them in centres where they live in security and companionship. The NGO works closely with forest departments to end the poaching of wild animals and works at educating and providing vocational training and alternative livelihoods to the communities traditionally involved in bear entertainment.

The royalty from this book goes towards supporting Wildlife S.O.S. With each book sold, we get one step closer to ensuring that bears like Beboo and her brother remain in the wild, where they belong.

To help save India's bears and wildlife, you may donate online at www.wildlifesos.org.

WOULD YOU LIKE TO HELP BEARS LIKE BEBOO AND OTHER WILD ANIMALS?